ཉིན་རེའི་ཞལ་འདོན།།

Daily Recitations

LIBRARY OF TIBETAN WORKS AND ARCHIVES

Sixth revised edition 1993
Reprint 1998
LIBRARY OF TIBETAN WORKS AND ARCHIVES

ISBN: 81-85102-56-2

Published by the Library of Tibetan Works and Archives, Dharamsala, and printed at Indraprastha Press (CBT), 4 Bahadurshah Zafar Marg, New Delhi – 110002

༄༅། །འདི་ག་བོད་ཀྱི་དཔེ་མཛོད་ཁང་དུ་ནང་ཆོས་སློབ་སྦྱོང་དོན་གཉེར་གནང་མི་རྣམས་ལ་མཁོ་ཕྱིར་ཉིན་རེའི་ཆོས་ཀྱི་འཛིན་གྲྭ་དང་། འཆར་ཅན་རེས་གཟའན་ཀྲྭ་བ་ནས་འབྱེལ་གྱི་སྤྱི་དོའི་སྐྱོམ་སྦྱོང་ཆོས་ཕུན་བཙས་པའི་སྤོན་འགྲོའི་ཞལ་འདོན་དང་། སེམས་སྦྱོང་གི་སྤོན་དུ་ཚོགས་གསོག་ཡན་ལག་བདུན་པ་མཆ་ཡ་དང་བཅས་པ་འབུལ་དགོས་རྣམས་བོད་ཡིག་དུ་ནག་འགྲོས་སུ་ཕྱོགས་བསྒྲིགས་ཀྱིས་བྱུར་བགོད་ཐོག་དེ་དག་གི་སྐ་དོན་རྣམས་དབྱིན་ཡིག་ནང་ཚ་ཚང་བསྒྱུར་བསྒྲིགས་ཀྱི་བོད་དབྱིན་ཡན་སྦྱར་གྱི་རྒྱུན་འབྱེར་བལྟ་བདེའི་དཔེ་དེབ་འདེ་བཞིན་བོད་ཀྱི་དཔེ་མཛོད་ཁང་ནས་ཆེད་དུ་དཔར་འདེབས་བགྱིས་པ་ཡིན་གཤིས། འདེས་ཀྱང་མཁན་ཁྱབ་མར་གྱུར་སེམས་ཅན་རྒྱུད་ཀྱི་དུག་གསུམ་ས་བོན་དང་བཅས་པ་དུང་ནས་ཕྱུང་སྟེ་ཐེག་མཆོག་བསྟན་པའི་སྙིང་པོ་རེས་འབྱུང་། བྱང་ཆུབ་ཀྱི་སེམས། ཡང་དག་པའི་ལྟ་བ་རྣམ་པར་དག་པ་རྒྱུད་ལ་འབའི་རྨག་ཏུ་སྙེས་ཏེ་འགྲོ་ཀུན་སྟེན་བྲལ་སྐུ་བཞིའི་གོ་འཕང་རིན་པོ་ཆེ་མྱུར་དུ་འཐོབ་པའི་སྐྱེན་འདུན་བཅས། འཕགས་ཡུལ་ཏེ་མ་ཐལ། བཤུགས་སྐྱར་ང་རམ་ས་ལའི་བོད་ཀྱི་དཔེ་མཛོད་ཁང་ནས། དཔར་ཐེངས་དུག་པ། བོད་རྒྱལ་ལོ་ ༢༡༡༨ མི་ཡོས། ཕྱི་ལོ་ ༡༩༩༡ ཟླ་ ༡༠ ཚེས་ ༢༡ ལ།། ༎

FOREWORD

This sixth edition of the "Daily Recitations of Preliminaries" is published by the Library of Tibetan Works and Archives for the benefit of those who are interested in the study and practice of Buddhism. These Preliminaries are recited in the daily classes and the monday meditation sessions at the Library for the purpose of training the mind and accumulating merit. Presented here are the Tibetan, phonetic and translated versions of such requisite practices as the seven-branched rite, the mandala offering and so forth.

By the merit of this may the three poisons of delusion be uprooted from the minds of sentient beings as extensive as space. May everyone develop renunciation, Bodhichitta and a correct view of emptiness, the three principles of the Mahayana teachings. May they hereby quickly attain the four bodies of a Buddha free of the two obstacles.

GYATSO TSERING
Director.

ཐོག་མའི་འདོན་ཆོག

PRELIMINARY PRAYER

MANJUSHRI

༄༅། །བླ་མ་དང་མགོན་པོ་རྗེ་བཙུན་འཇམ་དཔལ་དབྱངས་ལ་ཕྱག་འཚལ་ལོ།།

lama d'ang gonpo je-tzun jam-pal yang-ła ch'ag-tsal-lo

གང་གི་བློ་གྲོས་སྒྲིབ་གཉིས་སྤྲིན་བྲལ་ཉི་ལྟར་རྣམ་དག་རབ་གསལ་བས།།

g'ang-gi lo-dr'o drib-nyi trin-dral nyi-tar nam-d'ag rab-sal wä

ཇི་སྙེད་དོན་ཀུན་ཇི་བཞིན་གཟིགས་ཕྱིར་ཉིད་ཀྱི་ཐུགས་ཀར་གླེགས་བམ་འཛིན།།

j'i-nye don-kun j'i-zhin zig-chir nyi-kyi t'ug-kar leg-b'am dzin

གང་དག་སྲིད་པའི་བཙོན་རར་མ་རིག་མུན་འཐོམས་སྡུག་བསྔལ་གྱིས་གཟིར་བའི།།

g'ang-d'ag si-pai tson-rar ma-rig mun-t'om dug-ngal gyi-zir
wai

འགྲོ་ཚོགས་ཀུན་ལ་བུ་གཅིག་ལྟར་བརྩེ་ཡན་ལག་དྲུག་ཅུའི་དབྱངས་ལྡན་གསུང་།།

dro-tsog kun-la bu-chig tar-tze yan-lag dr'ug-chui yang-dän-
sung

འབྲུག་ལྟར་ཆེར་སྒྲོགས་ཉོན་མོངས་གཉིད་སློང་ལས་ཀྱི་ལྕགས་སྒྲོག་འགྲོལ་མཛད་ཅིང་།

drug-tar cher-drog nyon-mong nyi-long lä-kyi chag-drog drol-
dzä ching

མ་རིག་མུན་སེལ་སྡུག་བསྔལ་མྱུ་གུ་ཇི་སྙེད་གཅོད་མཛད་རལ་གྲི་བསྣམས།།

ma-rig mun-sel dug-ngal nyu-gu j'i-nye chö-dze ral-dri-nam

གདོད་ནས་དག་ཅིང་ས་བཅུའི་མཐར་སོན་ཡོན་ཏན་ལུས་རྫོགས་རྒྱལ་སྲས་ཐུ་བོའི་སྐུ།།

dö-nä dag-ching sa-chui t'ar-son yön-tän lü-dzog gyal-sä t'u
woi ku

བཅུ་ཕྲག་བཅུ་དང་བཅུ་གཉིས་རྒྱན་སྤྲས་བདག་བློའི་མུན་སེལ་འཇམ་དཔལ་

chu-tr'ag chu-d'ang chu-nyi gyän-trä dag-loi mun-sel jam-pal

དབྱངས་ལ་འདུད།།　　ༀ་ཨ་ར་པ་ཙ་ན་དྷཱི༔

yang-la-dü　　　OM A RA PA TSA NA DHI

བརྩེ་ལྡན་ཁྱེད་ཀྱི་མཁྱེན་རབ་འོད་ཟེར་གྱིས།།

tse-dän ky'ö-kyi ky'en-rab wo-zer-gyi

བདག་བློའི་གཏི་མུག་མུན་པ་རབ་གསལ་ནས།།

dag-loi ti-mug mun-pa rab-sal nä

བཀའ་དང་བསྟན་བཅོས་གཞུང་ལུགས་རྟོགས་པ་ཡི།།

ka-d'ang tän-chö zhung-lug tog-pa-yi

བློ་གྲོས་སྤོབས་པའི་སྣང་བ་སྩལ་དུ་གསོལ།།

lo-rdö pob-pai nang-wa tzal-dúu-sol

4

MANJUSHRI

Obeisance to my Guru and Protector, Manjushri,
Who holds at his heart a scriptural text
    symbolic of his seeing all things as they are,
Whose intelligence shines forth as the sun,
    unclouded by delusions or traces of ignorance,
Who teaches in sixty ways, with the loving compassion of a
    father for his only son,
    all creatures caught in the prison of samsara,
    confused in the darkness of their ignorance,
    overwhelmed by their suffering.
You, whose dragon-thunder-like proclamation of Dharma
    arouses us from the stupor of our delusions and free us
    from the iron chains of our karma.
Who wields the sword of wisdom hewing down suffering
wherever its sprouts appear,
    clearing away the darkness of ignorance.
You, who have been pure from the beginning who have
    completed the stages achieving the highest perfection of a
    Bodhisattva.
Whose princely body is adorned with the one hundred twelve
    marks of a Buddha

I bow down to you Manjushri.

(Manjushri's Mantra)

OM A RA PA TSA NA DHI

O compassionate one!, with the brilliance of your wisdom,

Illuminate the darkness enclosing by mind.

Enlighten my intelligence and wisdom so that I may gain insight

Into Buddha's words and the texts that explain them.

OFFERING TO THE ASSEMBLY OF BUDDHAS

ས་གཞི་སྤོས་ཀྱིས་བྱུགས་ཤིང་མེ་ཏོག་བཀྲམ།།

sa-zhi pö-kyi j'ug-shing me-tog-tram

རི་རབ་གླིང་བཞི་ཉི་ཟླས་བརྒྱན་པ་འདི།།

ri-rab ling-zhi nyidä gyän-pa di

སངས་རྒྱས་ཞིང་དུ་དམིགས་ཏེ་དབུལ་བ་ཡིས།།

sang-gyä zhing-du mig-te ul-wa-yi

འགྲོ་ཀུན་རྣམ་དག་ཞིང་ལ་སྤྱོད་པར་ཤོག།

dro-kun nam-dag zhing-la cho-par shog

ཨི་དམ་གུ་རུ་རཏྣ་མཎྜལ་ཀཾ་ནིཪྻ་ཏ་ཡ་མི།།

i-dam gu-ru rat-na mandala kam nir-ya ta-ya-mi

BUDDHA, MAITREYA AND ASANGA

འདྲེན་པ་མཉམ་མེད་སྟོན་པ་བཅོམ་ལྡན་འདས།།

dren-pa nyam-me tön-pa chom-dän-dä

7

རྒྱལ་ཚབ་དམ་པ་རྗེ་བཙུན་མི་ཕམ་མགོན།།།

gyal-tsab d'am-pa je-tzun mi-p'am-gön

རྒྱལ་བས་ལུང་བསྟན་འཕགས་པ་ཐོགས་མེད་ཞབས།།།

gyal-wä lung-tän p'ag-pa t'og-me zhab

སངས་རྒྱས་བྱང་སེམས་གསུམ་ལ་གསོལ་བ་འདེབས།།།

sang-gyä j'ang-sem sum-la sol-wa deb

BUDDHA, MANJUSHRI AND NAGARJUNA

སྨྲ་བ་བླ་མེད་འདྲེན་མཆོག་ཤཀྱའི་ཏོག

ma-wa da-me dren-ch'og sha-kyai-tog

རྒྱལ་བའི་མཁྱེན་རབ་ཀུན་འདུས་འཇམ་དཔལ་དབྱངས།།།

gyal-wai ky'en-rab kun-dü jam-pal-yang

ཟབ་མོའི་དོན་གཟིགས་འཕགས་མཆོག་ཀླུ་སྒྲུབ་ཞབས།།།

zab-moi d'ön-zig p'ag-ch'og lu-drub-zhab

སྨྲ་བའི་གཙུག་རྒྱན་གསུམ་ལ་གསོལ་བ་འདེབས།།།

ma-wai tsug-gyän sum-la sol-wa-deb

8

ARYADEVA

མགོན་དེའི་གདམས་པས་གོ་འཕངས་མཐོར་གཤེགས་ནས།།

gön-tei dam-pä go-p'ang t'or-sheg-nä

ཉིད་ཀྱིས་གཟིགས་གང་འགྲོ་ལ་གསལ་མཛད་པའི།།

nyi-kyi zig-gang dro-la sal-dze-pai

ལེགས་ལམ་སྟོན་པའི་གཏམ་ལ་དབང་འབྱོར་པ།།

leg-lam tön pai tam-la wang-jor-pa

འཕགས་པ་ལྷ་ཡི་ཞབས་ལ་གསོལ་བ་འདེབས།།

p'ag-pa lha-yi zhab-la sol-wa-de

CHANDRAKIRTI, VIDRAKOKILA THE ELDER AND YOUNGER

འཕགས་པའི་དགོངས་པ་གསལ་མཛད་ཟླ་བ་གྲགས།།

p'ag-pai gong-pa sal-dzä da-wa-dr'ag

རྒྱལ་སྲས་ཐུ་བོ་རིག་པའི་ཁུ་བྱུག་ཆེ།།

de-sä tu-wo rig-pai k'u-j'ug ch'e.

9

རྒྱལ་སྲས་རིག་པའི་ཁྱུ་མཆོག་གཉིས་པའི་ཞབས།།

gyal-sä rig-pai k'u-j'ug nyi-pai zhab

རིག་པའི་དབང་ཕྱུག་གསུམ་ལ་གསོལ་བ་འདེབས།།

rig-pai wang-ch'ug sum-la sol-wa-deb

SHANTIDEVA

གང་གི་མཚན་གྱི་འོད་ཟེར་ཆ་འས་ཙམ།།

g'ang-gi tsän-gy'i wozer ch'a-shä-tzam

སྐལ་ལྡན་ནུ་བའི་ལམ་དུ་ཞུགས་མ་ཐག།

käl-den na-wai lam-d'u zhug-ma:t'ag

སྙིང་གི་མུན་པ་སེལ་མཛད་རྒྱལ་བའི་སྲས།།

nying-gi mun-pa sel-dzä gyal-wai-sä

ཞི་བ་ལྷ་ཡི་ཞབས་ལ་གསོལ་བ་འདེབས།།

zhi-wa lha-yi zhab-la sol-wa-deb

HIS HOLINESS THE DALAI LAMA

རྒྱལ་ཀུན་སྙིང་རྗེའི་རང་གཟུགས་པད་དཀར་འཆང་།།

gyäl kun nying-jei rang-zug pä-kar-ch'ang

འགྲོ་བའི་དོན་དུ་གངས་རིའི་མགོན་པོའི་ཚུལ།།

dro-wai t'ön-t'u g'ang-ri gön-poi-tsul

བསྟན་འཛིན་ལྷ་གཅིག་འགྲོ་བའི་གཏན་གྱི་སྐྱབས།།

tän dzin lha-chig dro-wai tän-gyi-kyab

བསྟན་འཛིན་རྒྱ་མཚོའི་ཞབས་ལ་གསོལ་བ་འདེབས།།

tän dzin gya-tsoi zhab-la sol-wa-deb

THE LINEAGE GURUS

རབ་འབྱམས་གསུང་རབ་ཀུན་ལ་བལྟ་བའི་མིག།

rab-jam sung-rab kun-la ta-wai mig

སྐལ་བཟང་ཐར་པར་བགྲོད་པའི་འཇུག་ངོགས་མཆོག།

käl-sang t'ar-par drö-pai jug-ngog-ch'og

བརྩེ་བས་བསྐྱོད་པའི་ཐབས་མཁས་མཛད་པ་ཡིས།།

tze-wä kyö-pai t'ab-k'ä dzä-pa-yi

གསལ་མཛད་བཤེས་གཉེན་རྣམས་ལ་གསོལ་བ་འདེབས།།

säl-dzä she-nyen nam-la sol-wa-deb

11

དཔལ་ལྡན་བླ་མའི་རྣམ་པར་ཐར་པ་ལ། །

päl-dän la-mai nam-par t'ar-pa-la

སྐད་ཅིག་ཙམ་ཡང་ལོག་ལྟ་མི་སྐྱེ་ཞིང་། །

kä-chig tzam-yang log-ta mi-kye-zhing

ཅི་མཛད་ལེགས་པར་མཐོང་བའི་མོས་གུས་ཀྱིས། །

chi-dzä leg-par t'ong-wai mö-g'ü kyi

བླ་མའི་བྱིན་རླབས་སེམས་ལ་འཇུག་པར་ཤོག །

la-mai j'in-lab sem-la jug-par shog

OFFERING TO THE ASSEMBLY OF BUDDHAS

By the virtue of offering to assembly of Buddhas,
Visualised before me, this Mandala built on a base
Resplendent with flowers, saffron water and incense,
Adorned with Mount Meru and the Four Continents,
As well as with the Sun and Moon,
May all sentient beings share its effects.
Idam Guru Ratna mandalakam Niryatayami

BUDDHA, MAITREYA AND ASANGA

Buddha is unequalled as a teacher and a guide. The venerable protector Maitreya will be his successor. The exalted Arya Asanga has been prophesied by Buddha. From you three Buddhas and Bodhisattvas I request inspiration.

BUDDHA, MANJUSHRI AND NAGARJUNA

Buddha, head of the Shakya clan, is the foremost guide, peerless in expounding emptiness. Manjushri is the epitome of the Buddhas' complete wisdom. The exalted Nagarjuna, best of the Aryas, has seen the full meaning of profound emptiness. From you three crowning jewels of clear exposition I request inspiration.

ARYADEVA

Having reached a high state by following your master's instructions, you have shown wandering beings what have

seen. You were authorized to reveal the excellent path-
at your feet, Aryadeva, I request inspiration.

CHANDRAKIRTI, VIDYAKOKILA THE ELDER AND YOUNGER

Chandrakirti has elucidated the theme of Arya Nagarjuna's
teachings. The great Vidyakokila the Elder has been his
spiritual son. The exalted second Vidyakokila has been a true
Bodhisattva. From you three lords of wisdom I request
inspiration.

SHANTIDEVA

As soon as even a glittering syllable of the name of the
Bodhisattva Shantideva enters the ears of fortunate ones, it
eliminates their mental darkness.
From the exalted Shantideva I request inspiration.

HIS HOLINESS THE DALAI LAMA

O holder of the white lotus, embodiment of all the
conqueror's compassion, who appears as guide of the land of
Snow Mountains for the sake of wandering beings, you are
the sole deity and refuge of beings. At your feet, Tenzin
Gyatso, I request inspiration.

THE LINEAGE GURUS

These Gurus, moved by loving compassion, make the

14

Dharma clear by teaching with skilful and effective means. They are the best bridge for all those of good fortune to cross to liberation and the eyes for seeing all the vast scriptural texts, from all you Gurus I request inspiration.

May I never develop, for even a moment, wrong views towards the deeds of my glorious Gurus. With faith and respect gained from seeing their goodness, may the Gurus' inspiration flow into my mind.

༄༅། །སེམས་སྦྱོང་སྐོམ་གྱི་སྟོན་འགྲོ།

ཡན་ལག་བདུན་པ་མཊྫལ་དང་བཅས་པ།

PRELIMINARIES FOR MIND TRAINING
SEVEN BRANCH RITE AND MANDALA OFFERING

PRAYER OF REFUGE AND MIND GENERATION

སངས་རྒྱས་ཆོས་དང་ཚོགས་ཀྱི་མཆོག་རྣམས་ལ།།

sang-gyä ch'ö-d'ang tsog-kyi ch'og-nam-la

བྱང་ཆུབ་བར་དུ་བདག་ནི་སྐྱབས་སུ་མཆི།།

j'ang-chub b'ar-d'u dag-ni kyab-su-ch'i

བདག་གིས་སྦྱིན་སོགས་བགྱིས་པའི་བསོད་ནམས་ཀྱིས།།

dag-gi jin-sog gyi-pai so-nam-kyi

འགྲོ་ལ་ཕན་ཕྱིར་སངས་རྒྱས་འགྲུབ་པར་ཤོག།

dro-la p'än-ch'ir sang-gyä drub-par-shog

(Three times)

TAKING REFUGE

ན་མོ་གུ་རུ་བྱཿ   ན་མོ་བུདྡྷ་ཡ།།

na-mo guru-byah   na-mo buddha-ya

ན་མོ་དྷརྨ་ཡ།།   ན་མོ་སངྒྷ་ཡ།།

na-mo dharma-ya   na-mo sangha-ya

19

PROSTRATION

དུས་གསུམ་གཤེགས་པའི་སངས་རྒྱས་ཀུན།། ཆོས་དང་ཚོགས་ཀྱིས་

d'ü-sum sheg-pai sang-gyä kun chö-d'ang tsog-kyi

མཆོག་བཅས་ལ།། ཞིང་རྡུལ་ཀུན་གྱི་གྲངས་སྙེད་ཀྱི།།

ch'og-chä la zhing-dul kun-gyi dr'ang-nye kyi

ལུས་བཏུད་པས་ནི་བདག་ཕྱག་འཚལ།།

lü-tü pä-ni dag-ch'ag tsal

OFFERING

ཇི་ལྟར་འཇམ་དབྱངས་ལ་སོགས་པས། རྒྱལ་བ་རྣམས་ལ་མཆོད་མཛད་པ།།

j'i-tar jam-yang la-sog-pä gyal-wa nam-la ch'ö-dzä-pa

དེ་བཞིན་བདག་གིས་དེ་བཞིན་གཤེགས།།

d'e-zhin dag-g'i d'e-zhin-sheg

མགོན་པོ་སྲས་དང་བཅས་རྣམས་མཆོད།།

gön-pa sä-d'ang chä-nam-ch'ö

DECLARATION

ཐོག་མ་མེད་ལྡན་འཁོར་བ་ནས།། ཚེ་རབས་འདི་འམ་གཞན་དག་ཏུ།།

t'og-ma me-dän k'or-wa nä tse-rab di-am zhän-d'ag-tu

བདག་གིས་མ་འཚལ་སྡིག་བགྱིས་པའམ།། བགྱིད་དུ་སྩལ་བ་ཉིད་དང་ནི།།

dag-g'i ma tsal dig-gyi-pa-am gyi-d'u tzal-wa nyi-d'ang-ni

གཏི་མུག་འཁྲུལ་པས་བདག་ནོན་ཏེ།། རྗེས་སུ་ཡིད་རང་གང་བགྱིས་པ།།

ti-mug tr'ul-pä dag-non-te je-su yi-rang g'ang-gyi-pa

ནོངས་པ་དེ་ནི་མཐོང་བགྱིས་ནས།། བསམ་པ་ཐག་པས་མགོན་ལ་འཆགས།།

nong-pa d'e-ni t'ong-gyi-nä sam-pa t'ag-pä gön-la-shag

REJOICING

སེམས་ཅན་ཐམས་ཅད་བདེ་མཛད་པའི།། ཕྱགས་བགྱིད་དགེ་བ་རྒྱ་མཚོ་

sem-chän t'am-chä de-dzä-pai t'ug-kye ge-wa gya-tso

དང་།། སེམས་ཅན་ཕན་པར་མཛད་པ་ལ།།

-d'ang sem-chän p'än-par dzä-pa-la

དགའ་བས་རྗེས་སུ་ཡིད་རང་ངོ་།།

ga-wä je-su yi-rang-ngo

REQUESTING THE TEACHING

ཕྱོགས་རྣམས་ཀུན་གྱི་སངས་རྒྱས་ལ།། ཐལ་མོ་སྦྱར་ཏེ་གསོལ་བ་ནི།།

ch'og-nam kun-gyi sang-gyä-la t'al-mo jar-te sol-wa-ni

སེམས་ཅན་སྡུག་བསྔལ་མུན་འཐོམས་ལ།། ཆོས་ཀྱི་སྒྲོན་མེ་སྤྱར་དུ་གསོལ་

sem-chän dug-ngal mun-t'om-la ch'ö-kyi drön-me bar-d'u-sol

BESEECHING THE BUDDHAS TO REMAIN

རྒྱལ་བ་མྱུ་ངན་འདའ་བཞེད་ལ།། ཐལ་མོ་སྦྱར་ཏེ་གསོལ་བ་ནི།།

gyal-wa nya-ngän da-zhe-la t'al-mo jar-te sol-wa-ni

འགྲོ་འདི་སྟོངས་པར་མི་འགྱོད་ཅིང་།། བསྐལ་པ་གྲངས་མེད་བཞུགས་སུ་གསོལ།།

dro-di dong-par mi-gö-ching käl-pa drang-me zhug-su-sol

DEDICATION

དེ་ལྟར་འདི་དག་ཀུན་བྱས་ཏེ།། དགེ་བ་བདག་གིས་བསགས་པ་ལ།།

d'e-tar di-d'ag kun-j'ä-te ge-wa dag-g'i sag-pa-la

དེས་ནི་སེམས་ཅན་ཐམས་ཅད་ཀྱི།། སྡུག་བསྔལ་ཐམས་ཅད་བསལ་བར་ཤོག།།

d'e-ni sem-chän t'am-chä-kyi dug-ngal t'am-chä säl-war-shog

PRAYER OF REFUGE AND MIND GENERATION

I go for refuge, until I am enlightened. To the Buddhas, the Dharma and the highest Assembly.

From the virtuous merit that I collect by practising giving and other perfections,

May I attain the state of Buddha To be able to benefit all sentient beings

(Repeat three times)

TAKING REFUGE

I take refuge in my Gurus.
I take refuge in Buddha.
I take refuge in the Dharma.
I take refuge in the Sangha.

PROSTRATION

I prostrate before all the Buddhas who have come in the past, present and future, to the Dharma and the highest Assembly, the Sangha, bowing down with bodies as numerous as all the atoms of the world.

23

OFFERING

Just as Manjushri and other Bodhisattvas have made offerings to the Buddhas, so do I make offerings to the Buddhas and their protecting sons.

DECLARATION

From beginningless samsara, in this and other lives, I have unwittingly committed many non-virtues or caused others to do the same.

Bewildered by the confusion of my ignorance, I have rejoiced in my own and others' non-virtue. Seeing these mistakes, I declare all this to you protectors from the depth of my heart.

REJOICING

With happiness I rejoice at the ocean of virtues of developing the mind of enlightenment wishing to bring joy to all sentient beings and working for everyone's benefit.

REQUESTING THE TEACHING

With hands pressed together I request the Buddhas of all directions to light the lamp of Dharma for those who are groping in the darkness of suffering.

BESEECHING THE BUDDHAS TO REMAIN

These beings blinded by ignorance, have no one to guide them. O Buddhas, who might wish to pass beyond sorrow, I beseech you with hands pressed together please live for eons without number.

DEDICATION

By the merit I have gathered from all these acts of virtue done in this way, may all the sufferings of every being disappear.

OFFERING THE MANDALA OF THE UNIVERSE

ༀ་བཛྲ་བྷཱུ་མི་ཨཱཿཧཱུྃ༔   དབང་ཆེན་གསེར་གྱིས་ས་གཞི།

om vajra bhumi ah hung   wang-ch'en ser-gyi sa-zhi

ༀ་བཛྲ་རེ་ཁེ་ཨཱུ་ཧཱུྃ༔

om vajra re-khe ah hung

ཕྱི་ལྕགས་རི་ཁོར་ཡུག་གིས་བསྐོར་བའི་དབུས་སུ་རིའི་རྒྱལ་པོ་རི་རབ།

ch'i chag-ri k'or-yug-g'i kor-wai ü-su ri gyal-po ri-rab

ཤར་ལུས་འཕགས་པོ།   ལྷོ་འཛམ་བུ་གླིང་།   ནུབ་བ་ལང་སྤྱོད༔

shar lü-p'ag-po   lho-dzam-bu-ling   nub-b'a-lang-chö

བྱང་སྒྲ་མི་སྙན།   ལུས་དང་ལུས་འཕགས།   ང་ཡབ་དང་ང་ཡབ་གཞན།

j'ang dra-mi-nyän   lü-d'ang lü-p'ag   nga-yab d'ang nga-yab-
zhän

གཡོ་ལྡན་དང་ལམ་མཆོག་འགྲོ།   སྒྲ་མི་སྙན་དང་སྒྲ་མི་སྙན་གྱི་ཟླ།

yo-dän-d'ang lam-ch'ogdro   dra-mi-nyän-d'ang dra-mi-nyän-
gyi-da

རིན་པོ་ཆེའི་རི་བོ། དཔག་བསམ་གྱི་ཤིང༌། འདོད་འཇོའི་བ།

rin-po-ch'ei-ri-wo   pag-sam-gyi-shing   dö-joi-b'a

མ་རྨོས་པ་ཡི་ལོ་ཏོག འཁོར་ལོ་རིན་པོ་ཆེ། ནོར་བུ་རིན་པོ་ཆེ།

ma-mö-pa-yi-lo-tog   k'or-lo rin-po-ch'e   nor-bu rin-po-ch'e

བཙུན་མོ་རིན་པོ་ཆེ། བློན་པོ་རིན་པོ་ཆེ། གླང་པོ་རིན་པོ་ཆེ།

tsün-mo rin-po-ch'e   lön-po rin-po-ch'e   lang-po rin-po-ch'e

རྟ་མཆོག་རིན་པོ་ཆེ། དམག་དཔོན་རིན་པོ་ཆེ། གཏེར་ཆེན་པོའི་བུམ་པ།

ta-ch'og rin-po-ch'e   mag-pön rin-po-ch'e   ter-ch'en-pöi bum-
pa

སྒེག་མ། ཕྲེང་བ་མ། གླུ་མ། གར་མ། མེ་ཏོག་མ། བདུག་སྤོས་མ།

geg-ma   treng-wa-ma   lu-ma   g'ar-ma   me-tog-ma   dug-pö-ma

སྣང་གསལ་མ། དྲི་ཆབ་མ། ཉི་མ། ཟླ་བ། རིན་པོ་ཆེའི་གདུགས།

nang-säl-ma   dri-ch'ab-ma   nyi-ma   da-wa   rin-po-ch'ei dug

ཕྱོགས་ལས་རྣམ་པར་རྒྱལ་བའི་རྒྱལ་མཚན། དབུས་སུ་ལྷ་དང་མིའི་

ch'og-lä nam-par gyal-wai gyal-tsän   ü-su lha-d'ang-mi

དཔལ་འབྱོར་ཕུན་གསུམ་ཚོགས་པ་མ་ཆང་བ་མེད་པ་གཙང་ཞིང་ཡིད་དུ

päl-jor pün-sum tsog-pa ma-tsang-wa me-pa tzang-zhing yi-
du

འོང་བ་འདི་དག་དྲིན་ཅེན་རྩ་བ་དང་བརྒྱུད་པར་བཅས་པའི་དཔལ་ལྡན

ong-wa di-d'ag drin-ch'en tza-wa-d'ang gyü-par chä-pai pal-
dän

བླ་མ་དམ་པ་རྣམས་དང་། ཁྱད་པར་དུ་ཡང་བླ་མ་བློ་བཟང་ཐུབ་དབང་

la-ma d'am-pa nam-d'ang   ky'ä-par d'u-yang la-ma lo-sang
t'ub-wang

རྡོ་རྗེ་འཆང་ཆེན་པོའི་ལྷ་ཚོགས་འཁོར་དང་བཅས་པ་རྣམས་ལ་ཞིང་ཁམས་

do-je-ch'ang ch'en-poi lha-tsog k'or-d'ang chä-pa nam-la
zhing-k'am

དབུལ་བར་བགྱིའོ།། ཐུགས་རྗེས་འགྲོ་བའི་དོན་དུ་བཞེས་སུ་གསོལ།

ul-war gyi-o   t'ug-je dro-wai d'ön-d'u zhe-su-sol

བཞེས་ནས་ཀྱང་བདག་སོགས་འགྲོ་བ་མར་གྱུར་ནམ་མཁའི་མཐའ་དང་

zhe-nä-kyang dag-sog dro-wa mar-gyur nam-k'ai t'a-d'ang

མཉམ་པའི་སེམས་ཅན་ཐམས་ཅད་ལ་ཐུགས་བརྩེ་བ་ཆེན་པོའི་སྒོ་ནས་

nyam-pai sem-chän t'am-chä la t'ug tze-wa ch'en-poi go-nä

བྱིན་གྱིས་བརླབ་ཏུ་གསོལ།།

jin-gyi lab-tu-sol

* * *

ས་གཞི་སྤོས་ཀྱིས་བྱུགས་ཤིང་མེ་ཏོག་བཀྲམ།།

sa-zhi pö-kyi jug-shing me-tog-tram

རི་རབ་གླིང་བཞི་ཉི་ཟླས་བརྒྱན་པ་འདི།། སངས་རྒྱས་ཞིང་དུ་དམིགས་ཏེ་

ri-rab ling-zhi nyi-dä gyän-pa-di   sang-gyä shing-d'u mig-te

དཔུལ་བ་ཡིས།། འགྲོ་ཀུན་རྣམ་དག་ཞིང་ལ་སྤྱོད་པར་ཤོག།

ul-wa-yi   dro-kun nam-d'ag zhing-la chö-par-shog

* * *

སྟོན་པ་བླ་ན་མེད་པའི་བསྟན་པ་དང་།། མཇལ་བ་འདི་འདྲ་བླ་མའི་དྲིན་ཡིན་པས།།

tön-pa la-na me-pai tän-pa-d'ang jäl-wa di-dra la-mai dr'in
      yin-pä

དགེ་བ་འདི་ཡང་འགྲོ་བ་མ་ལུས་པ།། བཤེས་གཉེན་དམ་པས་འཛིན་པའི་

ge-wa di-yang dro-wa ma-lü-pa   she-nyen d'am-pä dzin-pai

རྒྱུ་རུ་བསྔོ།། ཨི་དམ་གུ་རུ་རཏྣ་མཎྜལ་ཀཾ་ནིརྻ་ཏ་ཡ་མི།།

gyu-ru-ngo   I-dam gu-ru rat-na mandala kam nir-ya ta-ya-mi

OFFERING THE MANDALA OF THE UNIVERSE

Om Vajra Bhumi Ah Hum
Here is the mighty and powerful golden base.
Om Vajra Rekhe Ah Hum
Here is the diamond-hard fence.
The outer ring is encircled with this iron fence,
In the centre stands Mount Meru, the King of All Mountains,
In the East is the continent Purva-vide
In the South Jambudvipa,
In the West Apara-godaniya,
In the North is the continent Uttarakuru
Around the East, the sub-continents Deha and Videha,
Around the South, Camara and Apara-camara, Around the
West, Satha and Uttara-mantrina, Around the North, the sub-
continents Kurava and Kaurava.
In the East is the Treasure Mountain,
In the South, the Wish-granting Tree,
In the West, the Wish-granting Cow,
In the North is the Unploughed Harvest.
Here is the Precious Wheel,
Here is the Precious Jewel,
Here is the Precious Queen,
Here is the Precious Minister,

Here is the Precious Elephant,
Here is the Precious and Best of Horses.
Here is the Precious General,
Here is the Great Treasure Vase,
Here is the Goddess of Beauty,
Here is the Goddess of Garlands,
Here is the Goddess of Song,
Here is the Goddess of Dance,
Here is the Goddess of Flowers,
Here is the Goddess of Incense,
Here is the Goddess of Light,
Here is the Goddess of Perfume,
Here is the Sun,
Here is the Moon,
Here is the Umbrella of all that is Precious,
Here the Banner of Victory in all the Directions,
In the Centre are all the possessions precious to gods and men
This magnificient collection lacking in nothing,
I offer to you, my kind and holy root Guru
Together with you venerable lineage Gurus,
And to you, Lama Je Tsong-kha-pa,
To you, O Buddha, and to you Vajradhara.
Together with the entire assembly of gods.

In your compassion accept what I offer for the sake of all beings. And after accepting them bestow on me please and on numberless mothers as vast as space, Your inspiration with loving compassion.

***

By the virtue of offering to you assembly of Buddhas
Visualized before me, this Mandala built on a base
Resplendent with flowers, saffron water and incense,
Adorned with Mount Meru and the Four

Continents, as well as with the Sun and the Moon.
May all sentient beings share its effects.

***

It is solely from the kindness of my Gurus
That I have come to be acquainted with the peerless Buddha's
   words;
Thus I dedicate this merit so that every sentient being
May be cared for in the future by kind and holy Gurus.

Idam Guru Ratna Mandalakam Niryatayami.
I sent forth this jewelled mandala to you precious Gurus.

MANTRAS

ཨོཾ་མུ་ནི་མེ་ནི་མཧཱ་མུ་ནི་ཡེ་སྭཱ་ཧཱ།།

om muni muni maha muni ye sva hung

སྨུཾ

mum

ཨོཾ་མ་ཎི་པདྨེ་ཧཱུྃ།།

om mani padme hung

ཧྲཱིཿ

hri

ཨོཾ་ཨ་ར་པ་ཙ་ན་དྷཱི།།

om wagi shwa ri mum

དྷཱི

dhi

ཨོཾ་བཛྲ་པཱ་ཎི་ཧཱུྃ།།

om vajra pani hung

ཧཱུྃ

hung

ཨོཾ་ཏཱ་རེ་ཏུཏྟཱ་རེ་ཏུ་རེ་སྭཱ་ཧཱ།།

om tare tutare ture sva-ha

ཏཱཾ

tam

33

MANTRAS	SEED SYLLABLES
Om Muni Muni Maha Muniye Svaha (Buddha)	MUM
Om Mani Padme Hum (Avalokitesvara)	HRI
Om Wagi Shvari Mum (Manjushri)	DHI
Om Vajra Pani Hum (Vajrapani)	HUM
Om Tare Tutare Ture Svaha (Tara)	TAM

༄ མཆོག་གི་བསྔོ་བ།

DEDICATION

ཕྱག་འཚལ་བ་དང་མཆོད་ཅིང་བཤགས་པ་དང་༎

ch'ag-tsäl wa-d'ang ch'ö-ching shag-pa d'ang

རྗེས་སུ་ཡི་རང་རངས་བསྐུལ་ཞིང་གསོལ་བ་ཡི༎

je-su yi-rang kul-zhing sol-wa-yi

དགེ་བ་ཆུང་ཟད་བདག་གིས་ཅི་བསགས་པ༎

ge-wa chung-zä dag-g'i chi-sag-pa

ཐམས་ཅད་རྫོགས་པའི་བྱང་ཆུབ་ཕྱིར་བསྔོའོ༎

t'am-chä dzog-pai j'ang-chub ch'ir-ngo-wo

***

གངས་རི་ར་བས་བསྐོར་བའི་ཞིང་ཁམས་འདིར༎

g'ang-ri ra-wä kor-wai zhing-k'am-dir

ཕན་དང་བདེ་བ་མ་ལུས་འབྱུང་བའི་གནས༎

pän-d'ang de-wa ma-lü jung-wai-nä

35

སྤྱན་རས་གཟིགས་དབང་བསྟན་འཛིན་རྒྱ་མཚོ་ཡི༎

chän-rä zig-wang tän-dzin gya-tso-yi

ཞབས་པད་སྲིད་མཐའི་བར་དུ་བརྟན་གྱུར་ཅིག༎

zha-pä si-t'ai bar-d'u tän-gyur-chig

***

སྟོན་པ་བླ་ན་མེད་པའི་བསྟན་པ་དང་༎

tön-pa la-na me-pai tän-pa-d'ang

མཇལ་བ་འདི་འདྲ་བླ་མའི་དྲིན་ཡིན་པས༎

jäl-wa di-dra la-mai dr'in-yin-pä

དགེ་བ་འདི་ཡང་འགྲོ་བ་མ་ལུས་པ༎

ge-wa di-yang dro-wa ma-lü-pa

བཤེས་གཉེན་དམ་པས་འཛིན་པའི་རྒྱུ་རུ་བསྔོ།

she-nyen d'am-pä dzin-pai gyu-ru-ngo

***

འདི་ལྟར་བགྱིས་པའི་རྣམ་དཀར་དགེ་བ་ཡང་༎

di-tar gyi-pai nam-kar ge-wa-yang

དུས་གསུམ་བདེ་གཤེགས་སྲས་བཅས་ཐམས་ཅད་ཀྱི།།

dü-sum de-sheg sä-chä t'am-chä-kyi

མཛད་པ་སྨོན་ལམ་མ་ལུས་འགྲུབ་པ་དང་།།

dzä-pa mön-lam ma-lü drub-pa-d'ang

ལུང་རྟོགས་དམ་ཆོས་འཛིན་པའི་རྒྱུ་རུ་བསྔོ།།

lung-tog d'am ch'ö dzin-pai gyu-ru-ngo

**

བསྟན་པ་རིན་ཆེན་མཆོག་གིས་མ་ཁྱབ་པའམ།།

tän-pa rin-ch'en ch'og-gi ma-ky'ab pa-am

ཁྱབ་ཀྱང་ཉམས་པར་གྱུར་པའི་ཕྱོགས་དེར་ནི།།

ky'ab-kyang nyam-par gyur-pai ch'og-d'er ni

སྙིང་རྗེ་ཆེན་པོས་ཡིད་རབ་བསྐྱོད་པ་ཡིས།།

nying-je ch'en-pö yi-rab kyö-pa-yi

ཕན་བདེའི་གཏེར་དེ་གསལ་བར་བྱེད་པར་ཤོག།

p'än-dei ter-de säl-war j'e-par-shog

DEDICATION

Whatever small virtuous merit I have gathered
From Prostrating, Offering, Declaring, Rejoicing, Requesting
   and Beseeching,
I dedicate this to attain Full Enlightenment.

***

O! Avalokiteshvara, Tenzin Gyatso.
The source of benefit and bliss
In the snow land of Tibet.
Please live until the end of cyclic existence.

***

It is solely from the kindness of my Gurus
that I have to come to be acquainted with the peerless
   Buddha's words;
Thus I dedicate this merit so that every sentient being
May be cared for in the future by kind and holy Gurus

***

Now I dedicate the virtues that I have gathered,
For the Buddha's insights and teachings to be always
   preserved.
And for the prayers and the deeds for the Buddhas and
   Bodhisattvas.
Of all the three times to be accomplished and fulfilled.

***

With my heart going out with great compassion,
In whatever directions the most precious teachings have not
   yet spread,
Or once spread have declined,
May I expose this treasure of happiness and aid.